IMAGES OF ENGLAND

GARSTON
REVISITED

IMAGES OF ENGLAND

GARSTON
REVISITED

GARSTON & DISTRICT
HISTORICAL SOCIETY

TEMPUS

Frontispiece: An early view of sailing ships in Garston Docks.

First published 2007

Tempus Publishing
Cirencester Road, Chalford,
Stroud, Gloucestershire, GL6 8PE
www.tempus-publishing.com

Tempus Publishing is an imprint of NPI Media Group

British Library Cataloguing in Publication Data.
A catalogue record for this book is available from the British Library.

ISBN 978 0 7524 4439 0

Typesetting and origination by NPI Media Group
Printed in Great Britain

Contents

Acknowledgements

This book would not have been published without the help of the many people who have loaned photographs and supplied information. Thanks in general are due to members of the Garston & District Historical Society, including the Committee, visitors to the society talks and exhibitions, and readers of the *Garston News*.

In particular thanks are due to Mike Axworthy, Nancy Barber, Hedley Barron, John and Vivienne Bateman, Rebecca Black, Audrey Boothby, Joan Bradley, Bernard and Margaret Brett, Robert Brown, Malcolm Cave, Geoff Chadwick, David Childs, Ted Davies, John Derbyshire, Kenny Ellis, Bernadette Evans, Madeline Evans, Roy Forshaw, Mike and Sandra Gavin, Dorothy Griffiths, Eunice Hawes, Ken Holding, Brenda and Albert Hughes, John Jackson, Bill Jones, Paul King, Jean Leadbetter, Roy Lovering, Eric McFerran, Mrs M. Newby, Pam Otten, Joyce Parry, Dorothy Pederson, Barbara Price, Margaret Purcell, Peter Rawlinson, Hilary Rigby, Geoff Roberts, Herman Roberts, Wendy Smith, Don Stephens, John Sturgeon, Dr Tinne, Bob and Pam Williams, Ena Williams, Jim Williams, Joan and Alan Wilson, Paul Young.

We are also grateful to Liverpool Record Office for use of photographs from the City Engineers' Collection and to Brian Wright of British Associated Ports for access to the large box of fine photographs in the Dock Office.

All the photographs in *Garston Revisited* are 'new', in that they are all different to those in the first *Garston* archive book; the only exception being the one below – the iconic image of the Parish church with the gas holder behind – which simply could not be omitted.

Garston & District Historical Society are always pleased to receive photographs as donations, or which can be borrowed and copied, to go into an ever-increasing archive – and who knows, there may one day be sufficient for a third book!

The iconic Garston image of the Parish church with the gas holder behind.

Introduction

In 1996, Garston & District Historical Society members compiled our first book of photographs of the area, entitled *Garston*. At the time, we were spoilt for choice for the number of excellent photographs that were submitted by our local community, and there were difficult choices about what to include and what to leave out. Also, since the publication of that first book, many new photographs have come to light that we want to make available to the whole of our local community. We were delighted, therefore, when Tempus contacted us with the proposal that we should produce a second book, to be entitled *Garston Revisited*.

Publishing these books of photographs is a fulfilment of one of the main aims of Garston & District Historical Society. The society was formed in 1979, when a group of interested people got together with the aim of researching the history of Garston and collecting archive material about our local area, including photographs, documents and various types of artefacts.

Since then we have built up an archive of this material and our avowed aim is to make this material available to the community through regular exhibitions. However, not everyone can get to our local exhibitions, and by publishing these books we are able to let people all over the world access our material.

Although modern Garston is a suburb of Liverpool, having been incorporated into the city in 1902, to many local people it will always be 'Garston Village'. In this new book we have included a whole new set of photographs of buildings, both domestic and industrial, which record the vast changes that have taken place since the beginning of photography. However a place is more than a set of buildings; these houses and factories are homes and workplaces for the people of Garston.

Originally, in the first half of the nineteenth century, the population was comparatively static, and many of the people of Garston and their fathers and grandfathers had been born in Garston and the adjoining villages. With the coming of new industries, however, significant numbers of people began to arrive from outside the area.

In the early nineteenth century, people crossed the Mersey from the Cheshire salt fields, on the 'flats' (boats) that brought rock salt over to be processed at Garston Salt Works, which moved here from Salthouse Dock in Liverpool. Other people came from Cornholme, on the Lancashire/Yorkshire border, with Wilson's Bobbin Works, which moved to Garston to take advantage of better transport links. Many Welsh people arrived from Swansea with the copper works. At the same time, the development of Garston Docks, and other industries such as the bottle works, the tannery, Francis Morton and the match works drew a workforce from far and near.

Well into the twentieth century, dairy farmers who came originally from rural areas like the Lake District continued to provide the industrial workers with milk and dairy products. In recognition of the human aspect of Garston, we have included many photographs of people as well as places.

The area of Garston included in this book covers that of the original Garston Urban District, before its incorporation into Liverpool in 1902. The boundaries are therefore Jericho Lane and Rose Lane to the north, the river Mersey to the west, the main line railway running through Mossley Hill, West Allerton and Allerton to the east and the boundary with Speke to the south.

We hope that you will enjoy travelling back in time to visit 'old Garston' and that *Garston Revisited* will give you a view of the people and places of the past.

Garston & District Historical Society Exhibition in February 2006 in the Historic Reading Room in Wellington Street.

RECAPITULATION OF THE EXTENTS.

The Wapentake of West Derby.

West Derby, ...	. 35*l.* 12*s.* 8*d.*
Wavertree, ...	. 4*l.* 9*s.* 1½*d.*
Thingwall, ...	. 13*s.* 4*d.*
Everton, ...	. 25*l.* 10*s.* 10*d.*
Great Crosby, ...	. 5*l.* 17*s.* 6*d.*
Garston, ...	. 1*l.*
Toxteth, Croxteth, and Simonswood, ...	. 8*l.* 8*s.* 10*d.*
Free tenants of the Wapentake, ...	. 9*l.* 17*s.* 7*d.*
Bailiff and perquisites of the Wapentake, . . .	. 6*l.* 6*s.* 8*d.*

Total, 103*l.* 4*s.* 11¾*d.*

Perhaps the earliest mention of Garston was in the 1297 *Recapitulation of the Extents of the Wapentake of West Derby.*

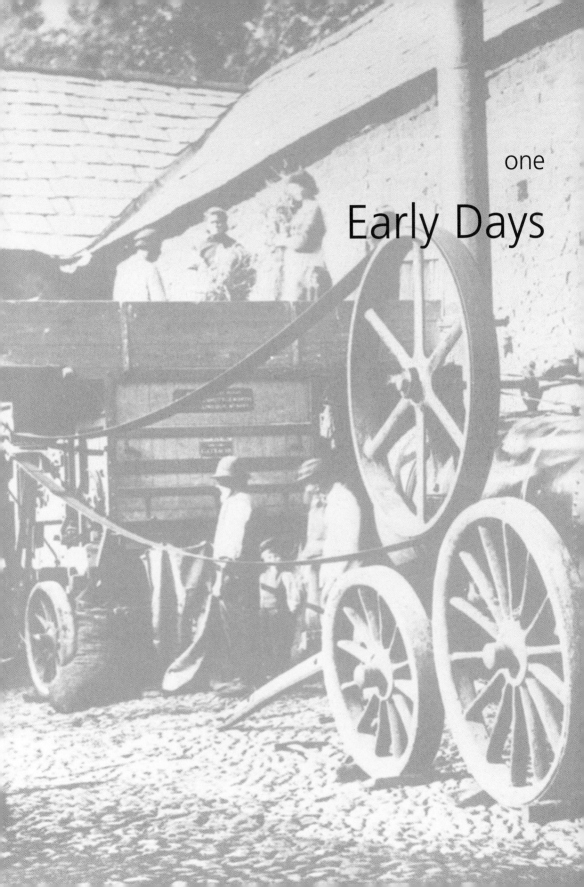

one

Early Days

This grainy photograph from 1870 must be one of the earliest of Garston and shows the original stone bridge in the background. On the right-hand side, the corner of the second church of St Michael, demolished in 1888, is visible.

The third church of St Michael from an 1887 painting by Jonathan Tushingham. To the left of the photograph is a similar view to that of the one above.

These people were gathering to watch the demolition, in the 1920s, of one of the old thatched cottages in the village at the corner of Speke Road and Church Road. In the background on the left can be seen the tower of the present St Michael's church and an industrial chimney – on the right, the new buildings on the opposite side of Church Road.

In July 1905, workmen replaced the old stone bridge with a stronger iron construction to carry freight engines and wagons to and from the docks.

Returning to the 1920s and the steel bridge can be seen above a Church Road busy with horse-drawn traffic.

A dust cart and horse belonging to Garston Urban District Council passing along Church Road next to the boundary wall of St Michael's church.

Horse-drawn carts again – this time in Heald Street, *c.* 1919. On the left-hand side of the road are the Winter Gardens. The white building on the right was the ambulance station during the Second World War.

Heald Street again, at the same date, with a wonderful old fire engine belonging to Liverpool fire brigade as this was nearly twenty years after Garston's incorporation into Liverpool.

The rear of the destructor building in 1903, looking towards the centre of Garston, with the sluice for the Garston river in the foreground. The sandstone wall in the foreground containing the sluice for the Garston river was part of the original mill dam. The destructor was built by Liverpool Corporation soon after the incorporation of Garston into Liverpool in 1902. Rubbish was burnt to an ash that could be used for road and concrete block making; the heat produced was used for generating electricity and heating moulds used for making concrete paving flags.

This is T.J. Mason's Cumberland Dairy in McBride Street in around 1907.

St Mary's Road, looking north, during the First World War – adverts leaning on the shop front read, 'send him a copy'. The shop with the canopy with the name 'Williams' is at No. 7. This was a grocer's and provision dealer's from the 1880s until the 1920s, the proprietor John Williams being eventually succeeded by Robert Williams (his son?). Somerfield supermarket's car park now occupies this site. Note the double, then single tram track going towards Aigburth.

St Mary's Road, looking south, with the Garston Hotel on the right. The photograph was a postcard sold by J.W. Dyble, a well-known tobacconist and stationery shop at No. 90 St Mary's Road from 1910 until the 1950s (originally John William Dyble then J.W. Dyble & Sons).

Above: Workmen queuing up for tea at Brook Farm on Woolton Road near Allerton station. The Mather Avenue trams used to terminate here, so the tea was popular with tram drivers and conductors. The Limacoat Factory was later built on the site.

Below: A threshing machine powered by a portable steam engine at Stanlawe Grange in the 1890s. The site is now occupied by Aigburth Nurseries.

Above and below: Two views of Garston Old Road, *c.* 1930. This road has changed very little in the intervening seventy years, the noticeable differences being the virtual lack of traffic and the demolition of the white building (White House Farm) on the extreme right of the picture below. In the background are the chimneys of St Mary's Terrace.

A tree-lined Aigburth Hall Road in 1898, seen from Cooper Avenue North. The wall and gateposts on the left are still standing, as is the large semi-detached house behind, whilst modern housing has been built behind the wall on the right of the roadway.

Another early shot – 1902 – this time looking down Mersey Road towards the river. The HSBC bank now stands on the left-hand corner. This was built in the 1920s and is the fourth building on the site; the first being the lodge of a thatched house called Briarley, the estate of which stretched down Mersey Road as far as the railway.

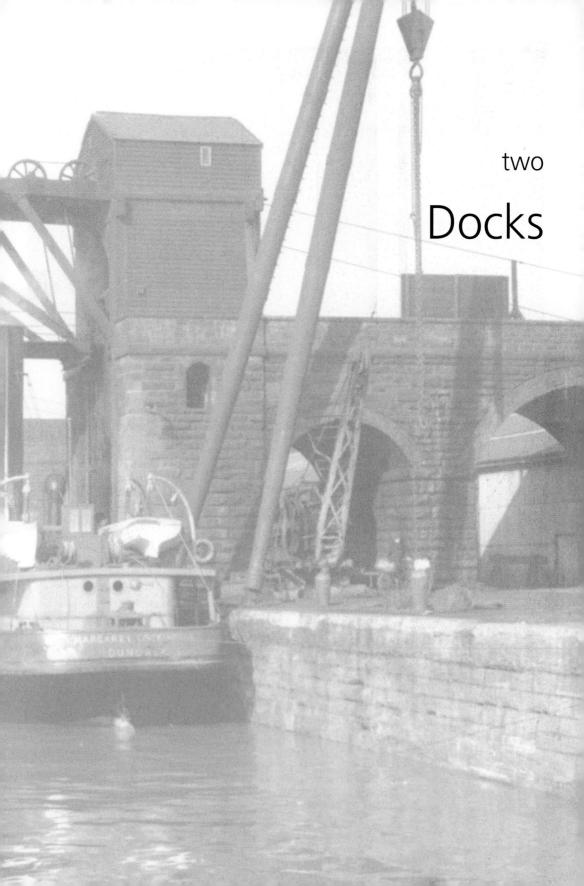

two

Docks

The Garston Dock complex consists of three docks, which originally had individual river access, but later was rationalised to the larger entrance at Stalbridge Dock. The first dock built was the centre dock called Old Dock, opened in 1846. The North Dock opened in 1867, and at the southern end, the largest Stalbridge Dock dates from 1909. The docks imported between 2 and 3 million tons per year in the first half of the twentieth century, whilst exports included 1 million tons of coal. The Old Dock has 2,160ft of berthing space, North Dock 2,400ft and Stalbridge Dock 3,170ft, with an entrance lock 276ft long and 65ft wide.

This view is taken from the bottom of Dock Road looking south at the Old Dock. Dock Road was the main access to the docks leading from St Mary's Road down to the Quayside. Originally called Bittocks Lane, this road was one of the main accesses to the shore before the building of the docks.

This view is of the stone-built coal drops on the North Dock with *Margaret Lockington* registered in Dundalk waiting to be loaded.

Above: The access to Garston Docks is via Garston Channel, which starts at the southern end of the Mersey Docks and Harbour Board system at Heculanium Dock. The upper reaches of the Mersey have always been prone to silting, the main reason why the docks moved from their original location in Widnes. This photograph, probably taken in the latter half of the nineteenth century, shows the bucket dredger which served Garston Dock, Garston Channel, Greenmore, Ireland and Deganwy, Wales excavating in the river Mersey.

Below: Lestris general cargo boat passes through the river entrance of Stalbridge Dock. Garston Old Dock and North Dock stretch into the distance over the access gates to the right of the boat. *Prince de Liege* (a banana boat) with a small tug follows on to enter the docks in the background. Elders and Fyffes banana sheds can be seen to the left.

The *Prince de Liege* was a war reparation ship, originally German, and was renamed the *Zent*.

Elders and Fyffes had an unloading berth on the river quayside of Stalbridge Dock, which, along with Southampton, received all the bananas imported into this country. Conveyors took the bunches directly from the hold of the ship into the warehouse, ready for dispatch in specially insulated railway wagons.

A photograph taken from the coal-tipping equipment on Stalbridge Dock looking across to the coal drops on the Old Docks Quayside. The Old Dock was the first railway dock built in Garston in 1846 and can be identified by its coal drops, which were originally timber structures later replaced by steel supports. The coastal trade was carried on 'steam puffers'.

The inauguration of the North Dock Container Terminal took place on Monday 26 July 1982, when the opening ceremony was performed by Malcolm Thornton, MP; it was to have a fairly short-lived service, and was later replaced by bulk cargo storage sheds. There is still a container depot next to the dock estate, although it is now used only as a road/rail interchange.

The London and North Western Railway Co. had ninety-three miles of railway sidings on the docks handling a variety of bulk cargoes such as coal, china clay and timber. Left uncontrolled, nature has always wanted to take over, as demonstrated by part of the former sidings today being declared a nature reserve. This photograph shows a weed-killing wagon drawn by a Wickham trolley on the coal sidings. In the background are colliery pit props imported into the docks ready for delivery by train to the St Helens' coalfield and beyond.

The dock gates were always vulnerable to damage. Storms raging down the river Mersey and vessels not always accurately manoeuvred damaged the gates on more than one occasion. Lock sluice gear also needed inspection and maintenance and there was always the possibility of a sunken obstruction in the one of the docks. This photograph, probably taken during the 1960s, shows a diver preparing to enter Stalbridge Dock.

Dock Office staff outside the Dock Office, *c.* 1880. Names on the photograph include Ashcroft, Houghton, Gregg, Roughley, Jones, Wood and Barber. The sign says that the office business hours are 8.30 a.m. to 5.30 p.m. weekdays, plus 8.30 a.m. to 1 p.m. on Saturday. A wage book at the time shows that annual salaries ranged from £30 to £300, with the majority of the staff receiving less than £100 per year.

Dock Office staff in the mid-twentieth century – dress code is still a suit, but they are no longer sporting the hats or caps of their nineteenth-century counterparts.

The coal drops at Garston were gravity-operated. The storage sidings were laid on an incline, which allowed the wagons to roll towards and away from the drops under their own weight. A hydraulic capstan pulled a rope, drawing the wagon onto the coal-drop platform. This was labour intensive, and the work included turning wagons, which were pointing in the wrong direction as the doors were only at one end. This posed photograph shows the wagon turntable on the Old Dock being operated, although the man standing between the rails is in danger of being knocked over. In the background can be seen the structure of another coal drop which emptied the contents of the wagons into the hold of the ship.

More smiling coal-drop staff posing for the camera.

The dock engineers' football team played their first game against the match works in 1954(5), winning 7-4. Left to right, back row: -?-, Bill Astbury, Albert Hughes, John Flusk, Edgar Ashcroft, Doug Wakefield, George Tittle, Cyril Whiteside, -?-, George Spencer. Front row: -?-, -?-, Les Harper, -?-, John Kinsey, -?-, Harry Hornby, -?-.

Ships in Stalbridge Dock, with famous Garston industrial landmarks in the background: the gas holder, the molasses tanks and the tannery.

three

Industry

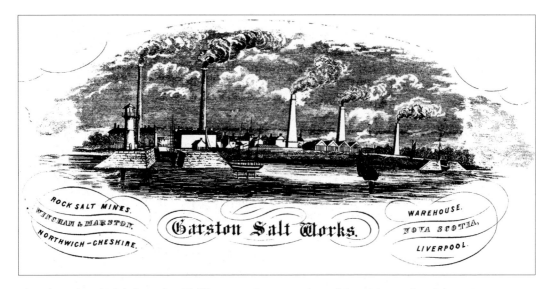

ROCK SALT MINES.

WINCHAM & MARSTON.

NORTHWICH-CHESHIRE.

Garston Salt Works.

WAREHOUSE.

NOVA SCOTIA,

LIVERPOOL.

The salt works, which belonged to Blackburne & Co., were relocated from Liverpool to Garston in 1798. Garston salt was celebrated for its superior quality and it continued to be made here until 1865, the output gradually diminishing to that date. As with the majority of the industries, which moved to, or grew up, in Garston, the attraction was the proximity of the river and Garston Docks. Rock salt was delivered from the Northwich area through the right-hand dock entrance and left after processing at the salt refinery by the left-hand dock. All traces of the salt works were removed in 1909 to establish the Stalbridge Dock.

Main entrance to the bobbin works in Blackburne Street. At the bottom of the tower was the time office. Above was one of several water tanks around the site, a precaution against fire. The hoses were hung up in the tower. There was also a reservoir by the wall along York Street. The building on the right was a dwelling occupied for many years by the caretaker and his family. All the machinery in the factory was designed to manufacture bobbins and shuttles for the textile industry and patented by Wilson Brothers, with maintenance carried out on site. In its heyday, 1 million bobbins per week were manufactured here. The factory closed in May 1958.

Members of Wilson Bobbin Works FC between 1946 and 1951 in the bobbin works' canteen.
Left to right, standing: Ken Williams, John Derbyshire, Fred Metcalfe, Albert Hughes, Len Threlfall,
Arthur Henderson, Ebor Thomas, George Mason, Jim Bennett, Ellis Derbyshire, Don McLeod,
Pat McDonald, Gerry Simpson, Ed Carruthers. Seated: Tommy Whelan, Stan Cheatham, Freddy
Williams, Ben Nicholls, Frank Trainor, Lenny Korish, Harry Burgess and Sam Derbyshire (who
was a life member of the club).

Bobbin works staff. Back row: R.J. Parry (second left), Mrs Jackson (seventh left). Front row: Mrs
Kitson (second left).

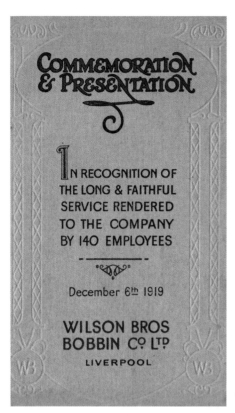

Left: 'Long Service' really was long at this 1919 presentation – ranging from a mere sixteen years for female workers Miss Maggie Eastaugh, Miss Annie Kelly, Mrs Beatrice Spencer and Mrs Martha Talbot (rancer, rabbeth borer, tube painter and tube marker respectively) to Mr John Jackson, a master turner, with forty-nine years' service. Other long service employees included John Holt, a tube rancer, Richard Kilkelly, sawyer, and Robert Williams, a counter, all with forty-six years' service. The longest-serving female employee was the office caretaker, Mrs Eaton who had worked for the firm for a quarter of a century, with twenty-nine men surpassing her achievement.

Below: Bobbin works office staff inside their office. They are, left to right: Bob Fleetwood, Elsie Rankin, Joyce Craig, Elsie Bailey and Jack Parry. Note the office equipment of the period.

Behind Garston Parish church can be seen the gas works, first built in 1891 as a Carburetted Water Gas Plant with a capacity of 4 million cubic feet per day. In 1910 an oil pipeline was constructed directly to the Stalbridge Dock. With the advent of North Sea Gas in the 1970s, the skyline changed dramatically as the site changed from gas production to gas storage only.

The main entrance to the tannery in King Street. The building on the right of the door was opened in 1911 for the drying and processing of 'bend' leather for the manufacture of footwear soles. The lower-level building on the left of the door was originally part of the iron foundry (Garston Iron & Steel Works). The rest of the tannery site was cleared in 2007 after closure in 2006.

Above: A crowd gathers on a bright sunny day to watch an amazing sight – the demolition of the Tannery Chimney by the late Fred Dibnah towards the end of the 1980s. Children from Banks Road School can be seen in the foreground with the headmaster Mr Garnett. Anyone recognise themselves?

Left: Going, going, gone!

Opposite above: Retirement presentation to draughtsman Mr Harry Saunders by J.D. Shepherd, the director of the Garston Bottle Co. (Rockware Glass) in 1968. Looking on are, left to right: David Bragg and Stan Tyson (draughtsmen), Jack Strollin (chargehand – fitting shop), Geoff Pennycook (apprentice draughtsman), Graham Glaister (works' engineer), Joe Rawlinson (draughtsman) and Geoff Chadwick (chief draughtsman), who was also presented with a watch by Mr Shepherd for twenty-five years of service with the same company.

By the end of the 1960s Garston Bottle Co. had become Rockware Glass, with its own fleet of lorries. Note all the crates of bottles behind the lorry.

Left: Indenture from the 15 January 1918 between Francis Morton & Co. Ltd of Garston and George Edward Childs, the son of George Childs, as apprentice plater: remaining term four years ten months of a seven-year apprenticeship.

Below: Christmas party for staff at Francis Morton (Garston) Ironworks, *c.* 1950 – Jim Williams Snr is seated on left at the end of the second table upwards: he worked at Morton's all his life. Also in the photograph are Harry Saunders and Joe Rawlinson, who worked at Morton's until its closure before starting work at Garston Bottle Co.

Above: Staff from Limacoat at a special evening at the Stork Hotel in 1961. Managers of the Famous Army Stores from all over the country attended. Staff on the front row include Jack Kermode, Harry Brown (retired works manager), Elsie Lawson, D.C. Wright (accountant), Mrs Morley, Tony Morley, F.H. Wilson, Austin Wilson, Mary Hill (secretary to F.H. Wilson), Bob Benjimin (solicitor), Pam Steiner (also secretary to F.H. Wilson), and Mr Morgan (cashier). The company, which made overalls and other work clothes, had a large contract with the Army and Navy Stores. It started on Speke Road at the corner of Horrocks Avenue on the site of the present job centre and later moved to Woolton Road near to South Liverpool's football ground.

Below: These employees of Grayson, Rollo and Clover Docks are about to board the charabanc for their annual outing. This photograph was taken at some time between 1950 and 1970. Tommy Dudley, who was a plumber, is standing fourth from the right and next to him (fifth from right) is Reg Williams, who was an engine fitter.

Left: Staff from the invoicing department of Mapleton's Nut Food Co. on the 29 May 1951. From left to right, back row: Barbara Gubbins, Betty Smith, Joan Dillon. Middle row: Doreen Wakeham, -?-. Front row: Audrey Smith, Sheila Robinson and Brenda Walker. Founded by Hugh Mapleton, the factory was opened in Moss Street in 1909 in premises which had been previously occupied by a sawmill run by Messrs J. Rawlinson & Sons. Hugh Mapleton had become a strict vegetarian and had found it difficult to obtain balanced and satisfying meals; he had the idea of making the nut the basis of these meals, and set up the company to produce them.

Below: Articles of apprenticeship for Robert Brown when he was apprenticed as a fitter to Bryant and May in 1956 for a term of five years. Note all the signatures and the Bryant and May Seal.

In Witness whereof the Apprentice and the Guardian have set their hands and seals and the Employer has hereunto affixed his Common Seal the day and year first above written.

Signed, sealed and delivered by the above named
ROBERT BROWN
in the presence of

Signed, sealed and delivered by the above named
FREDERICK BROWN
in the presence of

The Common Seal of BRYANT & MAY LIMITED, was hereto affixed in the presence of

Director.

Secretary.

SECRETARY

Manager.

Works.

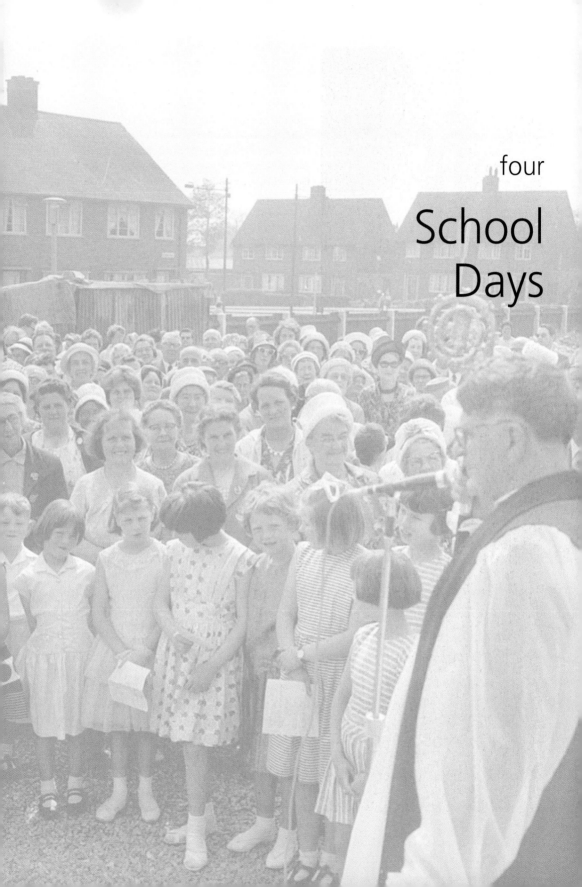

four

School
Days

'School days' for many Garstonians started early at the nursery in Banks Road. It was established during the 1920s and according to the 1930 Kelly's Directory was called the City of Liverpool Corporation Day Nursery with Matron Miss Bertha A. Dockey in charge. During the Second World War, the nursery provided a facility for looking after the children of the women engaged in war work. Mrs N.H. Thomas is listed as matron in 1949. It was renamed the Hilda Mason Nursery after the next matron, who was in charge from 1955 until she was tragically killed in a road accident in November 1978 when she was travelling home from work to the Wirral. Hilda Mason can be seen in the centre, in 1965, wearing a sister's uniform, with Audrey Connolly standing third left from her. They are in the prefabricated building, which was replaced by the present one adjoining the new village hall, both of which were constructed as part of the Millennium celebrations and were officially opened by Queen Elizabeth II in July 1999.

Above: Class 1 of St Mary's C of E School in 1978. Pupils are L. Hammond, A. Hornby, S. Crane, L. Jackson, K. Bates, Paul Ogden, A. Jones, Tony Graves, L. Martin, P. Ashcroft, I. ?, Andrea Morris, I. Hughes, T. Parkinson, P. Murphy, Philip Agate, C. Iles, Gerard E. ?, and Mark Williams. The teachers are M.R. Williams and L. Kilpatrick. In the background can be seen the building which was used for Island Road Wesleyan Methodist School from 1897 until the late 1920s. In recent years it has been used by many community organisations as part of Island Road Methodist church.

Right: Medal awarded to George Childs of the Victoria Public Elementary School in 1911 for 'marked regularity of attendance and general good conduct during four years'. The school, which was known at the time as Grassendale Victoria High Grade School, was built in 1898 and demolished in 1990, the majority of remaining pupils transferring to Garston C of E School in Holman Road for the autumn term of that year. A small development of sheltered housing now occupies the site.

Pupils from the same school in 1910, with Fred Varley standing (the fourth boy along from the female teacher). Fred lived with his family opposite the swing park, so he didn't have far to go to school!

Blessed John Almond School in 1964 – winners of the Everton Shield Football Competition. From left to right, back row: Mr Calvert, Gary Byrne, Paul Mullard, Steven McDonald, Edward Vose, Paul Caslin, Paul Johnson, John Sweeney. Front row: Eaunus McNulty, Michael Axworthy, Terry Williams and Michael Powney. Blessed John Almond School became St John Almond School (Comprehensive) in 1983 with the reorganisation of Catholic education in the city. It was renamed St Benedict's College in 2004.

Gathered for a reunion in the Central Hall of Banks Road School are ex-pupils, ex-teachers and guests, who contributed memories for a book about the school. Ex-pupils are William Hallam, Barbara Swain, Eddie Shuker, Marjorie Leadbetter, Jean McIntosh, John Derbyshire, Vera Norton, Gladys Norton, Edward Grace, Eva Crowther, William Cokersol, Nellie Jolly, Herman Roberts, Joan Barlow, Shirley Fogg, Thomas Barlow, and Jim Jones. Ex-staff are Mr Thomas, Shirley Smith, Miss Corrin and Mr Badham.

Standards 7 and 8 at Banks Road School, probably prior to the First World War.

Above: Were these girls in pretty dresses preparing for the May Day celebrations? This photograph was taken inside Banks Road School during the 1920s.

Below: To encourage punctuality and regular attendance, certificates were presented to children who achieved 100 per cent attendance. This was organised by Liverpool Education Committee and ceremonies were often held at St George's Hall, with children being granted a half-day holiday. This certificate was presented to Doris Stansfield in August 1911.

St Austin's R.C. School pupils in 1952. From left to right, back row: Gavin, Wally, Hunter, Barker, McCubery, Jones, Reynolds, Foley, Humphries, Janice, O'Connell, Pinnington, Wilson. Middle row: Cleary, Small, MacDonald, Martin, Simons, Dunn, Anderson, Evans, Morris, Hughes, Snelham. Front row: M. Murphy, V. Hughes, M. Shaw, B. Doyle, H. Keely, M. Laverty, E. Rowe, P. MacVeigh, P. Anson, J. Dowling, J. Hunter, P. Deagan, M. Riley, C. Hyde. At this time, classes were still taking place in the old school building (now Challoner Hall Social Club), before moving to the present buildings in Riverbank Road.

A smart-looking girls' class from Garston C of E School just after the First World War.

Garston C of E School in 1947. Left to right, back row: Fred Stimbson, Billy Darnell, Norman Green, Jimmy Kearns, -?-, Bernie Keene, Rodney Owens, Stan Lewis, Roy Newby, Jim Robinson. Third row: Teddy Newby, -?-, -?-, -?-, Joan Thourogood, Margaret Thorpe, -?-, Murial Gilman, Dot Squires, -?-, Arthur Taylor. Second row: -?-, Jean Lunn, -?-, Marian Morris, Betty Cliff, -?-, -?-, Ann Hughes, -?-, Doreen Peters, -?-. Front row: -?-, -?-, Colin Porter, Jimmy Voght, -?-, -?-, -?-. The teacher is headmaster Mr Facey.

In glorious sunshine on Saturday 8 June 1963 there was a procession along Horrocks Avenue to the site in Holman Road for the laying of the foundation stone for the new school buildings. The stone was laid by Gilbert Knowles Esq, in the presence of the Lord Bishop of Warrington and a large crowd of supporters.

The Bishop of Warrington addressing the crowd at the laying of the foundation stone. There was already a unique fundraising scheme in operation to help pay the Church's share of the cost of the buildings. On 29 January 1962, to a background of ships' sirens and the cheers of over 400 people, SS *The Brick Scheme* was launched. The work was explained as a building operation, and a clerk of works was appointed, and under him nine foremen. Over fifty brick setters offered their services there and then, and in all, 1,000 families pledged to give 6d weekly for every paper stamp 'brick' they bought. A total of over £10,500 was raised by the time the school opened for the summer term of 1964.

Gathered in front of Holy Trinity School in 1928 are Father McCarthy's 'Own' Scouts and Cubs. Apart from Father McCarthy, two others are identified as Peter Gavin (next but one left to the priest) and Jimmy Davies, seated next to Peter Gavin. Until 1964, when Garston C of E School was relocated to new buildings in Holman Road, there were three schools in Banks Road. Until 1944 they all catered for children from the age of five until the school leaving age of fourteen. They all had nicknames: Garston C of E School, formerly Garston National School (Nackers), was known as Cracked Eggs, Holy Trinity as Holy Tripe and Banks Road as Sausages. In the early part of the twentieth century, there was a huge increase in the school-age population of Garston, partly due to the fall in infant mortality, but mainly due to the increased opportunities for employment for families moving to Garston. In 1914 there were 1,220 children attending Banks Road School, 1,000 at the C of E School and around 800 at Holy Trinity, making a total of 3,000 at the three schools in Banks Road. Just imagine how busy it would have been at 9 a.m., lunchtime and 4 p.m., and how noisy it must have been at playtime.

Opposite above: These boys at Heath Road School in the mid-1930s, with their master, Mr Langley, include Billy Atchforth, Larry Ost, Norman Errington, Stan Sharrocks, Teddy Cliffe, Pip Edwards and Billy Gaffney.

Staff at Gilmour, Heath Road in 1963. From left to right, back row: Ronnie Wood (woodwork teacher), Dave Henry (modern languages), Len Taylor, Arthur Bunn. Middle row: Brian Thomas, Wally Jones, Brian Leeson, Arthur Upfold, Don Stephens (history), John Robinson (moved to the Choir School in Salisbury), John Gilbert Alexander. Front row: Jack Feast (P.E.), Ian Cobban, James Norris (deputy head and science), headmaster Norman Bridge, George Jameson (maths), Norman Davidson (english), Johnny Hughes (art). Mr Bridge moved on to become head of Yew Tree Comprehensive School and was the author of two books – one of which is called *My Liverpool Schools*.

Above: Pupils from St Francis on a day out, *c.* 1950.

Opposite above: At the outbreak of war in September 1939, many Garston children were evacuated due to the danger facing them from living in close proximity to Garston Docks. Here is a typical scene of the time at Mersey Road station. Note that they are all wearing name tags. In the centre holding the little girl is Mr Oates, manager of the Cheshire Lines Railway.

Opposite below: Children in a classroom at St Francis in around 1950 include Micky Millea, Barny Doolan, Kevin Gledhill, Jean Smith, Eileen Kane, Eddie Wilson, Owen Gargan, Jimmy O'Brien, Gerry Loftus, Alec Murphy, Micky Healey, Matt ?, May Ireland and Kathleen Durkin.

Below: Class 111b Duncombe Road Infants in 1926.

Gilmour, Duncombe Road Senior girls in 1933.

The signs say Duncombe Road School, 'Best Wishes for Christmas' and 'Group VI'. The girls, including Gladys Winkles, were pictured soon after the school opened in 1909 and were about twelve-thirteen years old.

Above: Pixies at Southbank School, which opened in 1938 to cater for children up to the age of seven, with the emphasis on play as well as learning.

Right: These Southbank infant children are looking happy at the prospect of playtime. The boy second on the right is Ken Holding.

View of Riversdale College outside the navigation and engineering block. In the far distance is the radio and electronics block. The college buildings have now been demolished and apartment blocks constructed, many of which have fine views over the river Mersey.

Riversdale College – students from all over the world studied navigation and maritime engineering in this engineering workshop.

Right: Miss Irene Isabel (or Mabel) Marsh was the founder and principal of the Liverpool Physical Training College, and one of the leading practitioners of physical training for women in the country. She began her career at the age of seventeen by taking a two-year course under Mr Alexander of Southport and then opened a class for women at Waterloo. Following interests in Bootle and Liverpool YMCA gymnasiums she added a class at Bedford Street. When this became too small, Miss Marsh acquired the estate at Barkhill Road, from where she ran her physical training college until her death in 1938 at the age of sixty-three.

Below: The outdoor swimming pool at I.M. Marsh College. The college is now a campus belonging to Liverpool John Moores University and has a fine indoor pool, which replaced the one pictured.

Handwritten on chalkboard:

AS FAR AS I CAN REMEMBER WE TRANSFERRED FROM THE WESLEYAN SCHOOL TO DUNCOMBE ROAD IN 1909, WHEN WE MARCHED IN PROCCESSION TO THE NEW TIN SCHOOL IT WAS SURROUNDED BY FIELDS. IT WAS A VERY GOOD SCHOOL WELL DISCIPLINED. HAPPY DAYS

Q. Wood

Above: A garden party and fête in 1933 in aid of the Soroptomist Club of which Miss Marsh was a member. Miss Marsh was very fond of the extensive gardens at Barkhill and employed two full-time gardeners.

Left: Finally, Queenie Wood writes about how much she enjoyed her school days, and the day the children were transferred from the Wesleyan School to Duncombe Road Tin School in 1909.

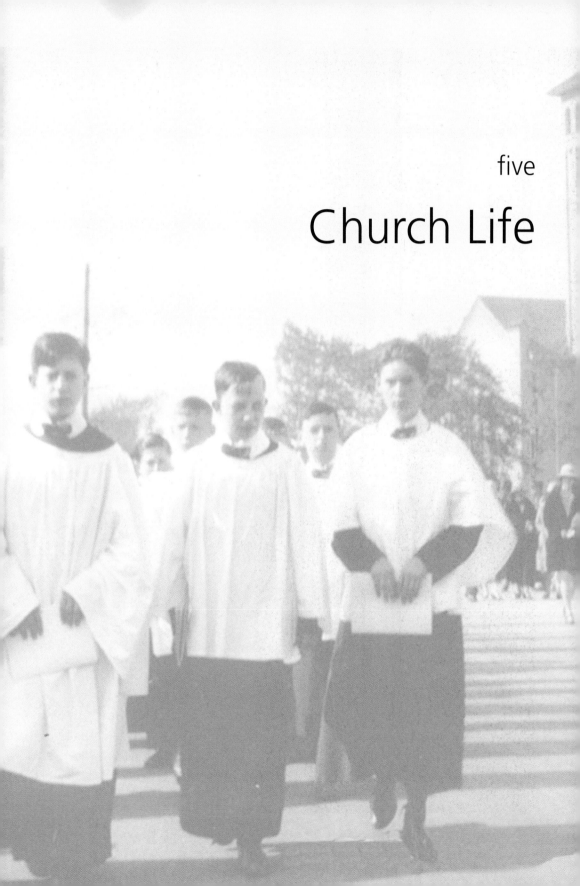

five

Church Life

- ADRODDIAD -

EGLWYS Y METHODISTIAID CALFINAIDD
CHAPEL ROAD.
GARSTON,
- Am y Flwyddyn 1929. -

Left: The Welsh Chapel in Chapel Road was opened in 1866 to serve the many Welsh people in Garston who had come with Bibby's Copper Works from South Wales. The chapel was sold in the 1980s and is now a private house.

Below: Ministers and elders of the Welsh Chapel, 1939/40. Left to right, back row: O.R. Williams, E.T. Edwards, Owen Owens, D.J. Patrick, Griffith Williams. Front row: Richard J. Jones, Revd John Daniel Evans and John Hughes.

The Welsh Mission Rooms in Canterbury Street are in the centre of the picture. In 1949 the building was sold to Liverpool Corporation. Other elders included R. Saunders Jones and R.J. Williams. The house on the left, on the corner of Derby Street and Canterbury Street, was occupied by a Mrs Lewis.

In 1928 (possibly on May Day) there was a fundraising event to raise money towards a new schoolroom for Wesleyan children. It took place on open grounds in Horrocks Avenue and also included dancing around the maypole.

Mather Avenue lined by soldiers. This procession was for the consecration of All Souls church on 21 May 1927 by the Lord Bishop of Liverpool, Dr A.A. David. People on the tram would have had an excellent view of the events.

The fine interior of All Souls church, the total cost of which was £25,000. Funding was received through the diocese, a legacy from Sir Alfred Jones and from fundraising amongst the new parishioners on the adjoining Springwood 'Economic' Estate. The style is Byzantine (320-1000 AD) and is one of the finest examples in the country. The architects were Messrs Campbell and Honeybourne of Liverpool.

An outing for members of the St Francis Parishioners' Guild in 1950. Standing, from left to right: –?–, Mrs Pegram, Mrs Gavin, Mrs Miller, –?–, –?–, Louise Rice, Julie Worrall. Seated: Mrs Warren, Mrs Foster, –?– and Miss Stott.

Members of Garston parish church's girls' gymnasium in 1912-13, who must have been very successful, judging by the number of medals pinned to their jumpers. On the far left is Grace Newbold.

Left: Ladies from Island Road Methodist church performing in a concert in 1927.

Below: Children from Garston Congregational church performing a traditional nativity play at Christmas 1958. This church, at the corner of Garston Old Road and Whitehedge Road, later became the United Reformed church and has recently amalgamated with Island Road Methodist church to become Garston Park church with the URC building now used as a school.

Amongst the members of the 6th Allerton Girl Guides in a performance of *Pollyanna* on the 2 November 1942 in the Congregational church are Dorothy Wilson, Joan Longworth (captain), Marjorie Simpson, Margaret Roberts, Nancy Parry and Joyce Parry.

An early Scout troop at camp; only some of the boys are wearing uniform, whilst the rest are in their ordinary clothes. Note the rope over the shoulders of those in the back row and the wonderful array of washing and cooking equipment in the foreground.

Above: A 1966 church parade passing Garston Parish church. The 6th Allerton Scouts are saluting the Lord Mayor, vicar and other dignitaries on a gloriously sunny day.

Below: Boys ready to take part in a much earlier 1929 Garston church parade, this time in Woolton Road, with the Number 8 tram in the background. Left to right: Leslie Owens, -?-, Reg Ives, Walter Owens and Lionel Walker.

Garston's Rose Queen, 14 June 1922 – a section of the procession is posing for the camera. Sam Ellis is the pageboy fourth from right.

Garston's Rose Queen, Doris Connor, and her retinue are gathered on a field near Holly Park, *c.* 1934. Allerton station is in the background.

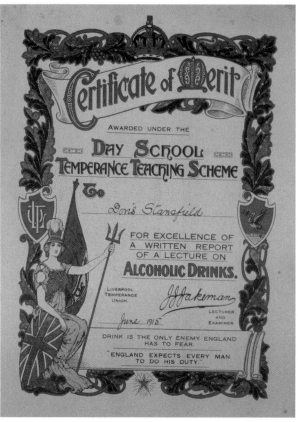

Above: Children from St Austin's church after taking their first Holy Communion in 1966. As most of these children attend St Austin's School, the boys wear their school blazers whilst the girls are wearing lovely traditional communion dresses.

Left: During the early twentieth century, the Temperance Movement was very strong and people were encouraged to 'take the pledge' and refrain from taking intoxicating liquids, with lectures being given in schools. Doris Stansfield was presented with this elaborate certificate, dated June 1915, for 'Excellence of a Written Report of a Lecture on Alcoholic Drinks'.

The Lord Mayor attended the church parade and service on 14 April 1991. His coach and horses are nearing the corner of Garston Old Road and Whitehedge Road.

Garston church cricket team, who were members of the Garston Cricket League. In the 1933 season they were runners up in the league and finalists in the Saunders Jones Cup. Standing on the right is Captain Lionel Walker.

To end this chapter, two productions: first, a play in 1941 in support of the United Nations.

Finally, an early amateur production (possibly *The Magic Key*) including Bob Whatling and Beryl Stopford. Note the authentic-looking long white beard.

six

Sport

Garston has a fine sporting tradition, which includes such famous sons as John Aldridge and Jimmy Case (football), Harry Fogg (water polo), John Parrot (snooker) and Austin Rawlinson (swimming), as well as the ladies from the 1920 British Olympic Swimming Relay Team. To start the sports section, here is one of the more unusual sports which took place in Garston – tug of war – with the tannery's team from the 1920s.

A more traditional sport, football, with this, the Banks Road FC team from 1906-7. 'Ned' Edward Davies is in the front row, kneeling on the left. He turned professional and played for Colne in the (then) Third Division.

A very successful Co-op Mid-week Football Team in 1958 after winning their league in 1956/7 and 1957/8 as well as being cup winners in the latter season. The photograph includes the officials and was taken at the West African Oil & Cake Mills Ground in Grassendale Road. From left to right, back row: Bob Lloyd, Frank Shannon, George Bromilow, Kenny Jackson, Les Ives, Harry Oakes, George Davies, Percy Roberts, Ronnie Edwards. Front row: Alex Jones, John Hennigan, Griff Jones, Billy Morehouse, Derek Mayers, and Cliff Bridges.

Silverdale Royal FC 1952/53. The team played on Garston Park and apparently were so named because one of the members had a caravan at Silverdale in the Lake District. From left to right, back row: Mr Tittle, Tommy ? , Mr Burton, Jones (married Winnie Tittle), -?- , Billy Baker, Billy Mercer, Georgie Tittle, Bobby Owen (Canterbury Street), Billy Atkins. Front row: Ray Burton (Window Lane), Jenkins, Kenny Burton, -?-, Ted Davies, Parr.

Trainer meets Nigerians.
The eighteen members of the Nigeria football team listen to their trainer, John Finch of Fulham F.C. upon arrival at Liverpool.

Above: South Liverpool 1949/50, winners of the Liverpool Challenge Cup, which they won at Goodison Park by beating Maghull 3-1. From left to right, back row: F.H. Wilcox, Vittles, Vance, Harry Woods, Ronnie Wright, Charles Swash. Front row: Bob Pringle, Miller, Frost, John Bennison, Ted Davies. Earlier in this season, on Wednesday 28 September 1949, South Liverpool FC played a visiting team from Nigeria, who famously played the match in bare feet!

Left: A section of the programme from the match.

GRAYSONS GARSTON F.C.

Pyke Cup Final 1922 – Grayson's Garston FC Mascot Sam Ellis, age seven, folding his arms in imitation of the team players. Sixth from the right on the back row, wearing a cap, is Percy Ellis, father of Sam.

Members of the Congregational Tennis Club in The Avenue, Garston. From left to right, back row: Win Parry, Stan Inch, Billy Hulme, Gordon Robinson, Fred Hughes, Leslie Robinson, Willis Clack, Gavin Walker. Middle row: Vicki Bird, Mary Robinson, Jean Dodd, Chrissy Hughes, Elizabeth Cuthbertson, May Jones. Front row: Jinny Hulme, Billy Walker, Lil Taylor.

These smiling faces belong to members of Holly Farm Cricket Club in 1933. Did the dog help with the fielding?

Holy Trinity Cricket Team, 1962. From left to right, back row: Pat Helbert, Brian Rowan, Paul McGlynn, Tommy Orr, Dave Killgallon, Norman Durcan, Tony O'Malley. Front row: Michael Powney, John Duffy, John Sweeney, Michael Axworthy, Amo Moore and Frank Durcan.

Rain stops play at Aigburth Cricket Ground. Liverpool Cricket Club, which is based here, celebrates its bicentenary this year (2007).

Horse-power at Liverpool Cricket Club, Aigburth Road. The magnificent pavilion is also shown in its full glory. During the First World War, the horse was kept in the house of a neighbour to prevent it being called up for war service.

The bowling green on Garston Recreation Ground at the corner of Garston Old Road and Island Road, with the rear of the houses of the latter at the top of the photograph. All the bowlers are resplendent in suits and hats.

The Bowls Express Cup winner in 1927-28 was T. Ellis, and the secretary for the event was Mr P. Rylands.

Garston District Bowling Team in the 1970s. Left to right, back row: Will Jones, Ralph Sherwood, Wilfred Moody, -?-, Peter Gavin and Bert Slater (next to right). Front row: Les Murphy (fourth left), -?-, Joe Quinn, Mo Hendrick, -?-. During the winter months the bowlers socialised in the 'Green Hut' between the swing park and Garston Park church.

Ladies from the Bowling Club, looking very glamorous.

Bob Whatling opening the bowling green at the LMS on Burnsall Street.

These young ladies were the winners of the rounders competition in 1910.

Up the Shore race, with runners Susan Bradley and Stephen Lee McDonald, which was organised for many years through Bankfield House.

Red Rum, the legendary winner of the Grand National, was the official starter of the 1991 Bankfield House Devil's Gallop and Up the Shore race. Vast crowds came to see the history-making horse, and one older lady, housebound for ten years, insisted on being there for the great occasion.

Above: Members of the Garston Swimming Club, *c.* 1920. Note the wonderfully stylish swimming costumes.

Left: The Olympic badge from the swimming costume worn by Austin Rawlinson at the 1924 Olympic Games in Paris – he was the only British finalist in the 100 metres backstroke and finished fifth. (The first six have their names placed on the Golden Roll of Honour of the games). He was also 150 yards backstroke champion of England from 1922-1926 inclusive. He later became the coach to the British swimming team for the European Championships in Budapest in 1958 and their team manager from 1959-1961, including the 1960 Olympic Games in Rome. In 1961 he was awarded the MBE for services to swimming.

Above: This team of swimmers were photographed in June 1966 at Garston Baths.

Right: This ornate certificate was presented to Olive Holding of Victoria School in June 1913 for swimming 50 yards breaststroke. She was also presented with an equally elaborate certificate for swimming 200 yards.

Garston Rifle Club.

The boxing Burns Brothers, twins Raymond and Paul, who were in the junior section, and younger brother Lee, who was in the schoolboy section at a Grand Amateur Boxing Tournament which took place at Garston Baths on 20 February 1986. The boys started boxing at Garston Amateur Boxing Club, which was located on the top floor of the Technical School building in Wellington Street. They were trained first by Charlie Stanley and then by Eddie Atherton and won local honours. Paul won the NABC Championship, represented England on twenty-six occasions and boxed for England in the Commonwealth Games before turning professional.

seven

Transport

Passengers leaving Church Road station, which was situated at the bridge in Church Road at the bottom of St Mary's Road, probably around the turn of the century. The occasion appears to involve some sort of procession or protest as there is a band, many men in railway uniform and the banner reads, 'Mersey Mission to Seamen and Railway Men'. At the time of the incorporation of Garston into Liverpool in 1902, there were surprisingly eight stations in Garston. They were Church Road, Dock Road, Garston and Allerton, as well as Otterspool, Mersey Road, Cressington and Mossley Hill.

Opposite above: The sign at Allerton station says 'Allerton for Garston', although there was a separate Garston station just a few hundred yards away. In recent years, the two stations have been demolished and the new South Liverpool Parkway erected as an interchange connecting the two different lines.

Opposite below: Those greeting Father Christmas at Speke Airport in December 1948 are Mr A.J. Hughes, Harry Ridman, Mr Lloyd and Mr J.P. Jones. Father Christmas is on his way to the children's party which was organised for the young relations and friends of Co-op staff.

Outside the Aigburth Hotel, *c.* 1907. This was an organised event where different kinds of vehicles were trialled against each other. In this photograph there are petrol and horse-drawn vehicles, whilst other photos in this series also contain steam-powered cars.

Again outside the Aigburth Hotel, with a coal cart in the background; the cyclists are standing between the horse tram tracks in the centre of Aigburth Road. The Aigburth Hotel was demolished as part of a road improvement scheme.

The first electric tram service in Liverpool was from South Castle Street to Dingle, with the first car and trailer leaving Dingle at 5.30 a.m. on the 14 November 1898. In 1900, the Garston & District Tramway Order granted powers for a line between Garston and Aigburth Vale together with a depot and a power station. The Number 45 tram is in Speke Road, *c.* 1951.

Speke Road bus shed in May 1955 after being converted into a drive-through fuel and oil bay.

Repairing the inner wall at the time of the construction of Garston Way, the Garston bypass, for which local residents had fought for many years and which would remove all the heavy lorries from St Mary's Road, thus improving conditions for residents, workers and traders in the village area. To the left is the Seamen's Mission.

On Sunday 15 January 1984 at 2 p.m., some 1,500 people braved the appalling weather conditions to walk along the Garston bypass prior to its official opening on the following day. The walk was led by the Pandemonium band, followed closely by Garston MP Eddie Loyden, members of Garston Community Council, City Council leaders and a contingent from Heald Street police station. Each person taking part in the walk was presented with a commemorative certificate.

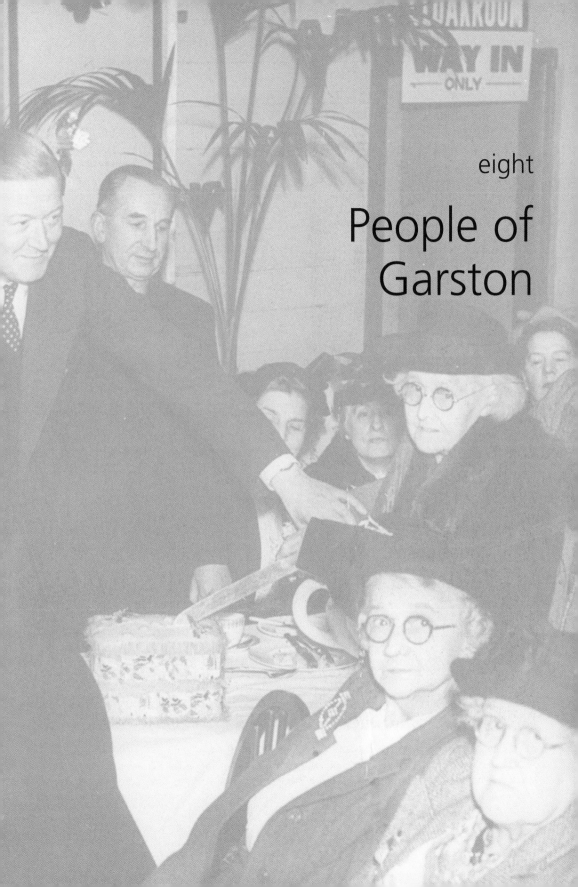

eight

People of Garston

The writing on the carriage reads 'J.H. Ramsbotham Valleyfield Farm, Aigburth Road – Tele 70 Garston'. The photograph was taken by The Carlton Studio, St Mary's Road, Garston, before the First World War. Fourth from the right is Percy Ellis, who was born in 1888. Valleyfield Farm was situated on Aigburth Road at the corner of Stratford Road.

William Bateman of Beechwood Farm with 'Floss' and Kenneth Kilgallon. This photograph was taken in Beechwood Road, c. 1953. Floss died on returning to the farm after completing a milk round. This made news in the local paper. Beechwood Farm stood in Beechwood Road opposite Liverpool Cricket Club. The buildings were demolished in 1988 when the family returned to Cumbria. Holmleigh Residential and Nursing Care Home now stands on the site.

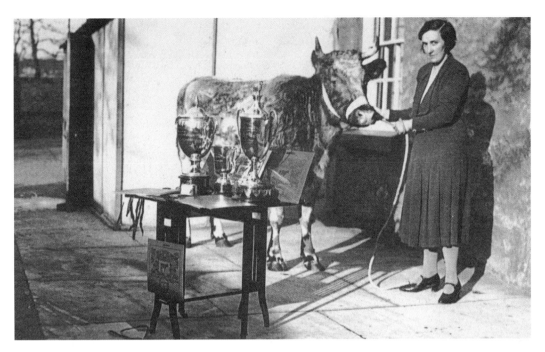

Mrs Molly Towers of Tower's Farm, Beechwood Road, with a prize-winning cow in 1933. The trophies on display had just been won at the show in Liverpool.

Edward and Gwen Towers with their young cousin Idonea (Ido) Barber and helpers. Edward is in his Quarry Bank School blazer. Tower's Farm in Beechwood Road started making and selling ice cream in 1934 just after Willie and Molly Towers purchased a Kelvinator machine from an exhibition in Liverpool.

These pretty fairies in Mrs Harris's garden, Grassendale Park are left to right, back row: Jean and Elsie Chesters, Maggie Howorth, Mary Craig. Front row: Linda Turner, Mabel Backshal, Mary Barry, Nellie Rimmer and Annie Ellis.

Residents of Sinclair Street in around 1935 are, left to right, ladies: Florrie Barnabus, Mary Agnes Clark, Mrs Kilgallon, Mrs Helbert, Mrs Illing, Mrs McNamara, Mrs Daly, Mrs Smith, Rosie Simmons, Gertie Scott and Mrs Barnabus (in front). Children: Tommy McNamara, May Docherty, John Tobin, Jimmy Barnabus, Chris McNamara and Mary Illing.

Passing along Window Lane is the funeral procession for William Hitchmough, who was buried in St Michael's church on 4 March 1909. Known as Billy the Barber, he had a shop in Window Lane. For a dare, he was reputed to have shaved a man in a lion's cage in Garston. Notice that most of the mourners are wearing bowler hats, although one has a Stetson and another just a cloth cap.

Garston LOL 64 Orange Lodge in the 1950s. The officers in the front row, left to right, are: W. Hughes (Snr), G. Gainey, W. Woods, C. Winckles, L. Peake, T. Foster, J. Parkes (Snr), F. Peake, J. Holt. The year 2007 is the centenary of the opening of the Victoria Hall in Heald Street, the home of the Orange Lodge, which was erected by Joseph Rawlinson's building firm.

Children are looking through the classroom windows at the teachers wearing some wonderful firemen's helmets. What was the occasion?

Were these boys photographed on the same day at the same school?

Members of the Woodcutters Club in the 1960s. From left to right, back row: ? Longbottom, Steve McGovern, Dyke Richardson, Arthur Holland, Paddy Walsh, Jimmy Wilkinson, Evan Jones, Billy Collet, -?-, Tommy Copoc, Joe Parry, Dick Ellis. Front row: founder members Jack Smith and ? Humphries, Jack Talbot, Mr Bewley (also a founder member) and Herbie Brodrick. The Woodcutters Club was founded in 1912 by wood machinists and sawyers from the bobbin works. They had a very famous band called The Woodcutters Novelty Band.

James Guinan is seventh from the right in this group of men ready to go on an outing in a 1950s-style Home James coach. Behind can be seen the Mona Castle pub at the bottom of the village and the sky appears to be full of overhead tram wires. It was probably an outing for members of the Woodcutters Club as James was secretary of the Garston Branch of The Amalgamated Society of Woodcutting Machinists, which was affiliated to the Joint Industrial Council of Bobbin and Shuttlemakers (Manchester and Radcliffe).

Michael Davies, aged eighty-eight, at the Wilson Hall being introduced to the Lord Lieutenant of Merseyside as being the oldest resident of Garston in 1955.

A group of men and boys outside the Ring 'O' Bells pub in Church Road; the building later became the premises for the famous Ingham's Cobblers.

Above: The sign held by the gentlemen in the centre reads, 'Palatine Picnic Party, Winsford, June 1960'. They are all sporting party hats and are gathered in front of the Home James coach in Island Road, close to the side of the Palatine pub. Note the gentleman in the grass skirt.

Below: Amongst the ladies about to go on an outing from the Canterbury are, back row: Sue Roberts (fifth from left), Grace McKenzie (on the right: she was a member of the Garston Relay Swimming Team in the 1920 Olympic Games). From left to right, middle row: Mrs Fletcher, -?-, Mrs Robinson, Mrs Chapman, Mrs Davies, -?-, -?-. Front row: Mrs Fairbanks (third from left).

Left: Two cousins, Norman Roberts and Albert Seafield, with their grandfather's carthorse, which is dressed for the May Day procession. This photograph was taken in the Corporation Yard, Garston Old Road in 1936.

Below: Enjoying a pint in the back parlour of the Alexandra pub are, left to right: Tom Cave, Sam Gill, Harry Wooding (dentist in Window Lane) and George Cave (a bottle worker). They were water polo fans and were members of the Garston Water Polo Team!

Above: Marie Axworthy and Julie Corns on Garston shore in the 1970s. In the background is the breaker's yard with boats belonging to the sailing club in front of the yard.

Below: By the river again, but this time Barbara and Charles Moody with their Auntie Betty (Ethel Elizabeth, née Moody) and Uncle Reg (Reginald) Vincent at a newly opened Otterspool Promenade in August 1952.

Cyclists at the corner of Meredith Street and Speke Road in 1948. Left to right: Charlie Jones, Albert Hughes, Alan Forrester, Maurice Rogers and Alan Peddar.

Postmen from Garston resplendent in their uniforms in 1907. They include J.P. Wilson (head postman), S. Parry (assistant head postman), J. Mercer (town postman), T. Freeman, H. Shone, J. Dowde, J.W. Bullock, J.J. Hartley, William Davies (Speke cycle postman), J.J. Grace (Speke Sunday postman) and S. Hart (Garston Sunday postman).

nine

Celebrations

Any excuse for a party! Garston celebrations ranging from festivities to celebrate the end of the Boer War, through the First and Second World Wars, George V's Silver Jubilee, and the present Queen's Coronation and Silver Jubilee. For many years, Garston held a carnival with a procession of decorated floats around Garston followed by events on Garston Park. Prizes were awarded for the best floats, and other competitions. This photograph is from the 31 May 1902, and shows locals celebrating the end of the Boer War. The large crowd is in front of Church Road Bridge – on the right St Michael's graveyard and, on the left, Railway Street.

Moving forward to the end of the First World War and this time a celebration tea party in Wharfdale Street.

Here in Canterbury Street in 1918, the majority of the boys seem to be more interested in the photographer than in the tea party.

Empire Day was celebrated in great style for many years. This occasion in 1938 at Holy Trinity School includes Teresa Mulholland, Mary Ashcroft, Dorothy Prince, Eddie Hogan, John Hogan, Terry Tipping, Alistair Brownbill, Peter Gunning, Maureen Cain, Patty Atkin, Gerald Bewley, Michael Kilkelly and Kenny Edwards.

Another celebration in the early part of the twentieth century.

Nearly every street in the country had a party to celebrate the end of the Second World War in Europe. The participants were virtually all women and children as they awaited the return of the men from military duty. However, as we know, many, who had made the supreme sacrifice, would not be returning. Firstly, the people of Etruria Street.

The residents of Calthorpe Street gathered, with flags flying, for their celebrations. Garston Park can be seen in the distance at the end of the road.

This time it is Condor Close. The lady in the white dress, standing before the front door in the centre, is Nellie Moody.

An 'Under the Bridge' children's party to celebrate Coronation day on 3 June 1953 was held at Garston Tannery because of rain! Among the children are Jimmy and Kitty State, Freddy Fox, Kevin Mullen, Tommy Healey and Alan Kuypers.

Wharfdale Street – and a party for the Coronation of Queen Elizabeth II in 1953. Could any of the older residents have been at the earlier 1918 party?

The people celebrating the same Coronation around the corner in Meredith Street are much younger.

Twenty-five years later and it is Queen Elizabeth II's Silver Jubilee. The lady in waiting on the left is Jacqueline Bradley and the girls are in Vineyard Street.

Garston Carnival was a local feature for many years with a parade of decorated floats through the streets ending on Garston Park, where there were stalls and fairground rides aplenty.

Garston Community Council

CARNIVAL
Float Award

1st Prize

Most Topical or ambitious

Grassendale Residents Association

Bernard G Brey —
CHAIRMAN OF COMMITTEE

Above: In 1978 the Grassendale Residents Association won first prize for the 'Most Topical or Ambitious Float', which was in the form of a Viking ship. Grassendale Residents Association was formed to prevent houses being built on the Lewis's Sports Ground in Ranelagh Drive North.

Right: Dressed for the occasion, from front to back, are Philip Wilson, Mark Wilson and Alan Wilson; Andy Flanagan is standing on the ship. The shields were made from decorated Liverpool 19 metal bin lids!

Left: Vikings Andy Flanagan and Norman Jones proudly holding their cups and certificates.

Below: The Great Garston Pram Race in 1985 – David Harwood is in the lead!

ten

Shops and Businesses

Above: Blacksmiths at Kettle Nook at around the turn of the century – one of them is Arthur Hornby.

Above: Staff outside the Long Lane branch of the Co-op: this shop was opened early in 1924 after extensive alterations to two houses, Nos 5 and 7 Long Lane, to form a shop, despite strong opposition from local residents. When completed it had a fine appearance with its attractive wall and railings in front.

Opposite below: Garston Co-op coal yard, *c.* 1920. Standing on the right of the picture is **Mr Percy Ellis**, the foreman. In its heyday, the Co-op also had shoe repair, window cleaning, hairdressing, and milk businesses as well as seven grocery stores and four butchers. In St Mary's Road alone in the mid-1900s, you could get a suit in the tailoring department at No. 63, furniture from No. 65 or visit the outfitters at No. 46 and the drapers at No. 82.

Right: The Co-op in Garston was established at a preliminary meeting on 1 April 1884 at Banks Road Mission Hall, when Mr Robert Wright, the headmaster of Garston National School, was voted chairman. The grocery and drapery departments, pictured, occupied Nos 80/82 St Mary's Road, which was a Co-op shop for over eighty years from 1890. In view of this, it is somewhat surprising that there is a 'Garston Co-operative Store' listed in St Mary's Road in the Kelly's Directory in 1862!

Above: A dinner for some of the staff employed by the Co-op in Garston, probably in the Winter Gardens in Heald Street, which later became a Co-op supermarket – one of the first in the area.

Left: Co-op delivery van with Joe Harper and his horse Lavender: both were well known in Garston for many years.

Opposite above: Silvers was firstly a milliner's and then a classy dress shop, trading at No. 44 St Mary's Road for over thirty years from around 1940. Left to right: Gladys Mays, Mrs Tauriger and Joyce Wilson (née Jones).

Below: Anne and Eric McFerran in their newsagent's shop in Church Road, which they ran for over thirty-five years, making it very much a part of the Garston community. It was, in fact, more than a shop, because you could get advice on all manner of subjects when you called in for your daily newspaper. In those thirty-five years, Eric also collected a large number of photographs and articles about Garston, which he was happy to share with Garston & District Historical Society.

Above and below: Smith's, at No. 12 St Mary's Road, was well known as a family business for over seventy-nine years, being established in 1907. It was started in James Street and then moved to the front of St Mary's Road and sold radios, cycles, records, toys and prams, and electrical goods. Above is a picture of the bottom end of St Mary's Road, with the H and V of the HMV sign above Smith's shop visible above the canopy in the centre of the shops on the left-hand side of the road. Below is a fascinating advertisement which appeared in the November 1929 edition of the *Springwood and Allerton Gazette* (Tenants' Association).

The sign on the hand cart reads 'Garston Family Laundry, Granville Road'. The occasion is unknown – but they are certainly not wearing their working clothes. Notice the dog as he also appears in the picture below.

The Garston Family Laundry's delivery van has some excellent signage on the side. The proprietor was J. Tranter and the business started in Mercer Street before moving to premises in Granville Road.

Above: A fleet of delivery vehicles for Garston Family Laundry with the laundry building behind. Note the wicker baskets which were used to transport the clean clothes and bedding.

Left: An advertisement for Dyble's tobacconist and newsagent's at No. 90 St Mary's Road, which shows the full and varied nature of their trade. It is Mr Dyble who we have to thank for the many postcards showing 'Old Garston' which have survived in the albums of local people.

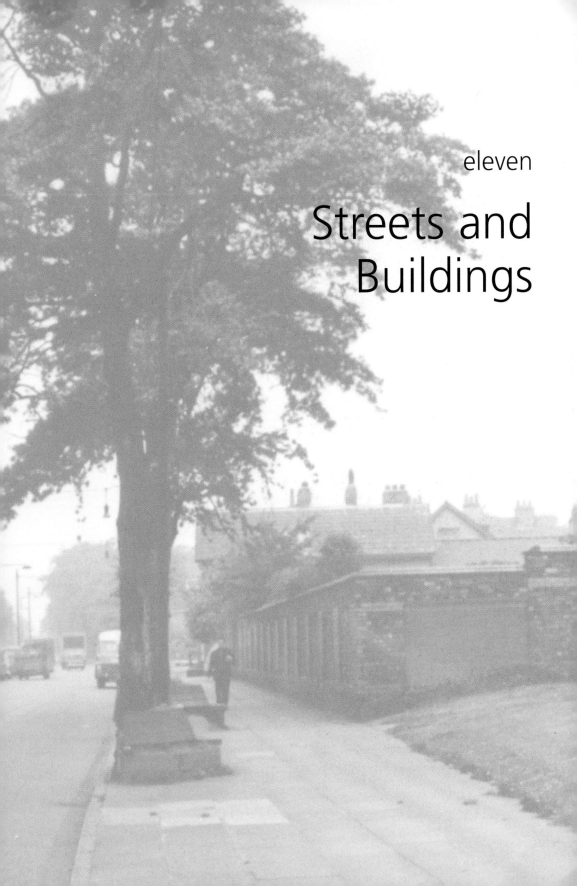

eleven

Streets and
Buildings

An aerial view of a section of Garston Park and some of the surrounding area. In the foreground can be seen the railway as well as Island Road, Clarendon Road, and Argyle Road. On the far side of the park is a tree-lined Long Lane with the Stamfordham 'Economic' Estate beyond. On the right is the junction of Mather Avenue and Woolton Road.

One of the prefabricated bungalows which were imported from America as a temporary measure to ease the housing shortage after the Second World War; many people will remember them on Garston Park alongside Long Lane. They were there for many years and were in fact very comfortable, having plenty of storage and even a small refrigerator.

Right: An ornamental drinking fountain on Garston Park: a cup made from enamel suspended from a chain provided the means, having pressed a button, to drink pure water.

Below left: A double ornamented lamp set on an island at the junction of Whitehedge Road and Garston Old Road. This started life as an oil burner, designed and invented by a man named Hastings who built all his lamps on islands as a refuge for pedestrians. They became known as Hastings Islands and date back to the 1890s.

Below right: One of the few old converted gas lamps on Cressington Promenade. The older men will remember throwing a rope over the arm of the lamps and making a swing. Very few of these lamps had the arms straight for long!

An early view of Grassendale Promenade, with its large elegant houses. This area has changed very little in the intervening years.

This postcard view of Allerton Cemetery states, 'Cemetery Entrance, Garston', although being situated on the far side of the railway line it is in fact in Allerton. It opened in 1909, after Liverpool Corporation purchased part of the Allerton Hall Estate to create a cemetery for South Liverpool, to solve the problem of a shortage of burial space.

Above: Laburnum Terrace in Chapel Road, next to the Welsh Chapel.

Below: Battlecrease House in Riversdale Road, at one time the home of cotton-broker James Maybrick, who died of arsenic poisoning; his widow Florence was tried and found guilty of his murder in 1889. The preliminary hearing of the case was held at the Reading Rooms in Wellington Street, Garston.

Aigburth Road by the Aigburth Hotel. The shops on the left are still standing, whilst the buildings on the right (as well as the fine tree) were sacrificed as part of the scheme for road-widening and dual-carriageway construction in the 1970s.

An early view of the entrance to La Sagesse School grounds, part of which has been retained to divide the new housing on the site from Aigburth Road.

Lincoln Street in the 1970s. This was one of the later streets constructed at the end of the nineteenth century, although plans to lay out the street had originally been placed before the Works and Health Committee of Garston UDC by the Garston Land Co. in June 1873.

Banks Road Recreation Ground in the 1970s. The land for this had been given to the people of Garston by Miss Watt of Speke Hall. On the left is Lyon Street and in the centre the imposing structures of the Banks Road School buildings – the Junior to the left and the Infants to the right. The Infants building was closed and demolished in 1993, the children being moved into the Junior building. A successful local campaign had prevented its planned closure ten years earlier.

A general view of a section of St Mary's Road in the 1960s: this is near to Clifton Street, looking towards the corner of Seddon Road. Some passengers are waiting at the stop for the 82A, 85 or 86 buses, whilst shoppers still have a good selection of shops from which to make their purchases.

James Street in 1969, with an excellent view of the impressive building which is the Swan public house on the corner of Wood Street. On the right the curved building is that of Caulfield's Pet and Pet Food Stores, well known to Garstonians and now converted into several individual houses.

The lychgate and section of the boundary wall of the present and third St Michael's (Garston Parish) church; they were constructed using the stone from the second parish church, demolished in 1888.

Finally, a view from the tower of St Michael's church taken in 1988: you can see the Blackburne Arms, Garston Old Mill and the site of the Mill Dam which was filled in by the railway company in 1907. Garston Docks are in the background. This whole area has recently been demolished with an archaeological dig taking place to uncover and record the foundations and remains of Adam de Gerstan's tanning and fulling mill, dating from the thirteenth century, and the Garston river, before redevelopment takes place. There is no doubt that Garston owes its development to this small river and mill as well as its proximity to the river Mersey.

Other local titles published by Tempus

Runcorn

H.F. STARKEY

This selection of over 200 archive photographs of Runcorn will fascinate all those who have ever lived or worked in the town. Many changes have occurred over this period of time; in this splendid sequence of images they are catalogued beautifully.

978 07524 3006 5

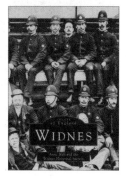

Widnes

ANN HALL

This fascinating collection of more than 180 archive photographs traces some of the many ways in which Widnes has changed over the last hundred years. A valuable historical record, this book depicts almost every aspect of life in the town as it used to be and will stir nostalgic memories in the minds of many readers.

978 07524 0117 1

Cheshire Life

MIKE EDDISON AND JOHN HOPKINS

Above all else, the county of Cheshire has been shaped by its people. These fascinating archive photographs combine views of the county with reminders of some of the people who have criss-crossed its landscape and left their mark. Representing all manner of Cheshire Life, the book will appeal to all those who know the area.

978 07524 4364 5

Mersey Voices

DIANA PULSON

Selected from local radio archives, this collection of personal memories provides a unique insight into the lives of all kinds of Merseyside people. They describe days long gone, the continual struggle to get by, events both comic and tragic, and finally give their thoughts on life in the new Millennium. They are a fitting reminder of how we lived in the twentieth century.

978 07524 1835 3

If you are interested in purchasing other books published by Tempus, or in case you have difficulty finding any Tempus books in your local bookshop, you can also place orders directly through our website

www.tempus-publishing.com